Dad had gone to London for an important meeting. He called Mum and sounded very excited. "Guess where I am going?" he said. "To Japan."

"Dad's going to Japan," Kipper told
Gran. "A company in Tokyo wants to use
the machine that Dad's company has
invented. Dad has to show it to them."

"Gran knows," said Dad.

"I do," said Gran. "I've had a good idea.
I'll pay for you *all* to fly to Tokyo."

"Wow!" said Biff. "Thank you! You are
the best gran in the world."

It was a long flight to Tokyo. It took over twelve hours.

"It's halfway round the world," said Biff.

"I'll be glad to get there," said Mum "You've all slept, but I haven't."

Mr Yamada met them at the airport. His wife Yoko and daughter Rio were with him.

"We are glad the children came with you," said Mr Yamada.

"Welcome to Japan," said Rio shyly.

"Rio is learning English," said Yoko.

"You look really pretty, Rio," said Mum.
"Is your dress called a kimono?"

"It's my summer kimono," said Rio.
"It's called a yukata."

"Now let's go to your hotel," said
Mr Yamada. "Tokyo is a very busy city.
It will take us about an hour to get there."

They were amazed when they saw the
hotel. It was very tall.

"Your rooms are near the top," said
Mr Yamada. "Tomorrow, Yoko and Rio will
be happy to take you sightseeing."

Biff and Chip took pictures of their hotel bedroom and sent them to Gran.

"It's an amazing room," said Chip. "We can see for miles across the city."

The next day, Yoko and Rio took Mum and the children sightseeing. The streets were very busy.

"Stay close to us," said Yoko. "You don't want to get lost."

They came to a huge toy store.

"Oh wow!" said Kipper. "Can we go in?"

"Not now," laughed Yoko. "It has five floors. We'd never get you out!"

They went to see a beautiful temple.
"It is the oldest temple in Tokyo,"
said Yoko.
"It's lovely," said Chip.

Paper lanterns hung at the entrance.
People stood in front of the temple to pray.

"Who are the men in robes?" asked
Kipper.

"They are monks," said Yoko.

There were little shops near the temple.
"Look at these lovely fans," said Biff.
"Let's buy one for Gran."
"That's a good idea," said Mum.

"It's time for lunch," said Yoko. "These are called bento boxes. Do you think you can use chopsticks?"

"The food looks such fun," said Kipper, "and I'll try to eat with chopsticks."

At last it was time to go back to the hotel.
But on the way to the station, they lost Yoko
and Rio.

"Oh dear," said Mum. "We had better try
and find the station by ourselves."

"Which way do we go?" said Mum.

At that moment, some school children stopped. They were excited about Kipper's fair hair.

"Do you speak English?" asked Kipper.

"Is it this way or that way?" said Mum.

"Don't worry, Mum," said Kipper. "My new friends will take us to the station."

"We use the train every day," they said.

They found Yoko and Rio at the station.

"Thank goodness you found your way here," said Yoko.

"Thanks to my new friends. I'm going to write to them when I get home," said Kipper.

The next day, the family set off on the bullet train to go to Kyoto. Rio and her parents came to see them off.

"Wow! Look at the train," said Biff. "It goes at 300 kilometres an hour."

On the train, the conductor inspected
tickets. When she got to the children she
smiled and pointed out of the window.

"You are lucky today!" she said.

Biff looked out and gasped.

In the distance was Mount Fuji.

"We *are* lucky," said Dad. "It's a clear day. It's not often you can see it."

The mountain was capped with snow.

"It's an amazing shape," said Biff.

"It is an active volcano," said Dad.
"That's why it is that shape."

"It won't erupt, will it?" asked Chip.

"The last time was in 1708," said Dad,
"so I don't think so."

In Kyoto, the hotel was different. It was a traditional Japanese inn.

"I love the bedroom," said Biff. "It is so different from the other hotel. We must take lots of pictures to show Gran."

"We are going to sleep on these mats, called tatami mats," said Dad.

"But on mattresses," said Mum. "And there's a wooden bath. It's to soak in. You must shower before you use it."

It was time to explore Kyoto.

"Kyoto used to be the capital city of Japan," said Dad. "One of its most beautiful buildings is the Golden Pavilion."

"Oh wow! It really is beautiful. Can we go inside?" asked Kipper.

"I don't know," said Mum.

A lady with a dog heard what Mum
had said.

"It is not possible to go inside," she said.
"Do you know that it is covered in real gold?"

In a part of the garden was a pot.
The kind lady told them it was lucky
to throw coins in it.

"May you always have good luck,"
she said.

At last it was time to fly home.

"I'll never forget our holiday in Japan,"
said Kipper.

"We *are* lucky to have seen all those
places in Tokyo and Kyoto," said Biff.

Gran met them at the airport.

"We have had a wonderful holiday," said Biff. "We can't wait to tell you all about it. Thank you so much, Gran."

The children spoke to Rio online.

"We still remember the Japanese you taught us, Rio," said Chip.

"Arigato – thank you!" Biff, Chip and Kipper all said together.